Root

Also by Linda Black:

Inventory

LINDA BLACK

Root

Shearsman Books

Published in the United Kingdom in 2011 by
Shearsman Books Ltd
58 Velwell Road
Exeter EX4 4LD

www.shearsman.com

ISBN 978-1-84861-170-2

Cover:
from 'Ribbons' (copperplate etching) by Linda Black.
Copyright © Linda Black, and reproduced with permission.

Acknowledgements:
Some of these poems have previously appeared in *Shearsman* Magazine,
Poetry Wales, *Tears in the Fence* and the online blog *Eyewear*.
My heartfelt thanks go to Mimi Khalvati, Esther Morgan,
Lucy Hamilton and Claire Crowther, all inspirational,
and of course to Tony Frazer.

Contents

II. Procreation

III. Exposure

IV. Emergence

Root

For my family – past, present and future

I.

Conception

The Onlooker: Encounter

Excuse me? She might say, but this would be later, this would be hindsight:

A disembodied voice, up and to the left, roughly in the same vicinity as her tinnitus. She is climbing the stairs, her stairs. Owned then: part carpeted, part extended, temporary nevertheless. A short journey, open to curtailment. She has chosen on this occasion for the walls either side paint with a slight sheen – harder, less susceptible. She is desirous of replacing the carpet, thinks; *the rolled up carpet* (100% wool, made in Belgium, Louis de B— predominately blue, beige, a bit of red – wasn't there a flood once? – part of it got so wet it wouldn't lie flat) *and other rugs*, hoping it will lead further. Yank it up. Start at the top and pull. Wisdom is external, floating slightly below the ceiling. *Speak to me then!* (If only she would listen.)

In order that she might complete what she had begun

Before what came next, she would have liked that it be a little earlier, say by an hour or so. What came next? (From the kitchen, the scraping of a spoon.) She cannot sit without thinking how to be better. She cannot abide. What she wants is that it may seem, when she leaves, she were never there. Nought to naught. No disturbance of cloth, no crease, no disarray. How inviting the plumped up cushions. Let them stay that way. Senses come unbidden, as does light, the importance of rhythm – and here a thought is strength, a desire a subordinate clause. Her need is for length: a thigh boot, an evening glove (each tiny button fastened tight), a scarf wending its way.

The kitchen is reached via a small flight of stone steps. The kitchen is below. She dips her fingers in a jug of water, splashes droplets purposefully across the fabric with a flick of her wrist.

A bow will do

This is not a new thought. Though it has specificity. Gold, or gilt, some cheap metal (which is not to devalue it) with its own particularity of shape, its own deception – beguiling, perfectly plausible. There are markings, patternings, an illusion of cloth or ribbon; something soft made hard. Entirely satisfying – in what? – in *suggestion*. More so than the real thing. From one illusion to another. Knowledge is in theory transferable. Knowledge in kind. Here she is, with a bow, a pre-existing bow about to be reinvented, again. The origin of a bow – is it possible to trace? This is about purity she thinks – or could be – or conception. Struggle and pleasure. How much she *wanted* to tie that shoelace. And then she could. Now she is misleading. She wants to get back to the bow. The flat, transitional bow. She could go downstairs right now, rummage and find it, but she doesn't want to. It isn't about a bow then, however you pronounce it.

She is unravelling a ball of cotton wool

This way it will go further. She peers over the top of her sewing glasses and her life is cut in half, allows her gaze to drift and soften. Light forms in wheels, legs on the chairs multiply.

She watches the other woman

The dark haired woman (she can't tell who came first) who is mending a blouse, thinks *I too have a blouse to mend*:

I am opening/to continue opening/to further open-up the side seam to add a zip, removing first the inadequate one, otherwise I can't get it over my head without a struggle, thus off. Mine is similar in shape and form, as is the one from which she snatches jet beads the size of knuckles, placed at regular intervals around the yoke. Transference. Why this endeavour? For a party I'm going to, replies the other woman. *Her party and I am not invited.*

Bringing out and putting away

Five times taken out and back un-done, many more in thought. Lay it ready on the bed – as time runs, put it again away. A failing hem, a pulled thread, a moth-hole on the flap of a pocket. A missing button somewhere saved for a rainy day.

Interpretation (1)

She recalls a conversation with a former friend (also with dark hair) – all that delving, trying to get to the bottom of it, bringing in of course one's life experience from which one has gleaned so much; such knowing, such authority, such ability to speak with wisdom about the lives of others, and after much deliberation, such *certainty*: discovering not long after it *wasn't even him* who'd walked straight past her in the street.

(Unsure of the time of day, she needs to get home, so she runs, scooping up the little one, so fast she misses where it is she lives, straight past, though surely it can't be far away, but where? turning lost and looking, from the inside now, along a corridor, down the stairs, for the way out, the house not quite her style but finished how she'd like hers to be, asking the way of a passerby, the map hard to interpret, not in her language though how should that matter? popping the little-one inside her cardigan for safe keeping, reaching the end of the road, directed by a man about to cross the same bridge, realising she's done this journey before, and all she can see ahead is an expanse not solid enough to walk on, so she leaps like surfing on air, arms splayed, propelling herself, the little-one still inside her cardigan, which is just as well, knowing if she reaches the phone box over the road she'll get the help she needs but the box is derelict, the door barred with planks of wood so how's she ever going to get where she's going? when she sees a bus-stop and a woman standing there offering to carry the both of them, turning just in time to spy a dark-haired woman holding a tiny child rushing past so fast she doesn't notice her at all.)

Apart at the seams

What is inside, enclosed, trapped in there (between those careful stitches)? How big or little can a purpose be? To get for example to the end of the path, to reach ones toes. What constitutes a treat? Everything is in a way on the way to something else. Everything on the way is in its own way something else, something else in the way, in its own way.

On the third morning of her acquaintance

With the dark-haired woman (for what cause, wonders The Onlooker, does she recall such an incident?) seated diagonally opposite at the breakfast table, a gesture – seemingly of no consequence, not a hint of malice nor any intention to provoke – accompanied by a request as innocuous as please to pass the sugar, elicits such a response as could not be anticipated in any of the self-help manuals on the hall table. (She has always thought herself not a resentful person.) And so it is, the matter not dropped, she finds herself unwittingly transformed into the other woman's father.

E J Arnold & Co, Stock No 201194

One page blank, one lined; lined (right), blank (left); lined front, blank back, reversed from the centrefold (blank, blank), the final page being lined (as is the first), each blue line – neither too dark or too pale – a pleasing distance (8mm) from the ones above and below. She hovers, inhabits the spaces between. Each blank page remains and will so remain. Each, by requirement, should have upon it a drawing in pencil or crayon in a child's hand: some aspect of desire, of a world seen not as wanting. Who knows the demeanour of those who wouldst populate such unruly realms?

The Onlooker dictates

Neither pen nor paper (to hand) nor any notion of such, this she ignores (as does he). Something in common? Patience/ desperation: action/stupefaction – I think not. He may very well reach the end before she ever begins. Take that page in a notebook (Stock Nº 201194) some way in: 'I never thought you'd get *this* far' her tutor had written, and she hasn't. Lines run through her head (the beautiful bounty of silence never hers) deeply wrought: chatter, mutter, matter, utter tripe – white, visceral, on a tray in the butcher's window. *Repeat after me.* How could anyone stomach it?

She feels sick

And as she leans forwards, wretched, retching, an image
– this would be an etching – begins to form: the symbolic
contents of her (add a few belongings) spewing from her own
wide mouth, caught in mid-stream; such precious artefacts,
a lifetime's worth, so fine and neatly drawn. How pretty a
picture would that be?

II.

Procreation

Traces

What she tries to recall is the impulse – call it inception. Does a precedent preclude, negate what comes next? She remembers a diagram (sort of): iron filings arranged (they do it themselves don't they?) in concentric circles, radiating from something central to which they are drawn, from which they repel. Something causal. Nothing to do with where she hopes to get. Do they have selves? How many does she?

The Onlooker makes an appointment

Tries to: give an inch and you get – nothing, beating about in the wind, the barrel. A bush orphan. Foolish to even try.

Strictures, heaps and piles of them remorselessly present find their leeway, leeching in (thank you for having me doesn't enter into it) – a chink, an opening (her eye half-shut) – unrestrained (one could say welcomed). Complicity, duplicity – always the circuitous route (along the ginnel, up the drainpipe – she wouldn't dare). All that wanting to want to – relinquishing not seizing. Phone a friend. Ask the audience.

Interpretation (2)

(A small van careers over a hump; doors fly open, rolled lengths of towel tumble, unfurling along the road. She rushes helpfully to retrieve them. After neatly refolding she steps indoors. The place, which isn't hers, is furnished with everything old, found, patched together. She is clearing up someone else's mess, wiping down the work surface with a dirty cloth; she opens intermittently odd drawers with broken fascias, looking for a clean one. By the side of the sink a small selection of fungi sprouts from a hollow.)

Not to her liking she likes it anyway this place where nothing matches, crammed with crocks, textiles, artefacts – not for her, which it isn't. A towel, grey as an old dishcloth, one end of it stitched to the other, hangs by the sink on a roller. So it must have been for a very long time: so it seems it will stay (of this she is certain). Judgement/difference (profound)/comparison: how one lives one's life: a certain admiration – else why would this woman appear to her in dreams as she has over the years? Representation/aspiration/creativity – expressed/unexpressed. Working artist/failure.

'Harpist'

Enters her mind so it should mean something. It's the same with 'Perlman' or *Perel*man. Her job is to delve. She knows 'perel' means pearl in Ashkenazi, but she wants more. It relates but it doesn't. The 'r' rolls around her tongue and when she speaks it she makes with it two syllables not one: Perél. Goodman, Lipman: one or other or both was the first name should-have-been-surname of the grandfather she never knew. What she knows is he had a little dog with short legs and ran a pub in Leeds, plying his customers with salt-herring – not a pearl in sight. Then she sees the closeness to peril and wonders is she taking the wrong tack. A connection to music would be pleasing but what it is evades her. She is diligent. She is trustworthy. She takes care. Care where care calls for. If she thinks of it – and she never has – she is made of such a strange mixture it is hard to be sure of anything. One-minute this one-minute that, neither more desirable than the other. Whatever this is or that is pushes from inside. She would like some added information: an amendment, a summing up, a plan, a plot, a synopsis, bullet points, an abbreviation.

All this harping on and no potatoes and the broccoli gone rotten.

Ten years previously

She writes of today: *It* she expects will go on: the bed will need changing, the cats if they are alive (they are not) need feeding; the bills will need paying. She postulates in similar vein about dust and paraphernalia, cites a generic white shirt (too clean to wash, not clean enough to re-hang) on the wardrobe door, mutating it into another along with a pair of shoes, the problem of the leaking roof equally interchangeable. Which of those she hasn't yet met won't want to hear from her? Who will she have cried for?

His father

Won't stop talking, making that noise – *boom-boom, va-voom* or some such phrase, over and over, even though she's asked him please to stop it, asked him once then again which is something she wouldn't usually do. He never did take any notice of her, covering the little ones' eggs in salt all those years ago, pouring spoonfuls of sugar into their cups of tea. Cups of tea! At their age! She can't concentrate. But he doesn't care – inside her head without an invitation.

She liked the space on the landing

Where the stairs turned as if it were extra, a place in which she might pause leaning her back against the wall, where the sun might shine as on the lawn at her grandparents' house, briefly; the lawn she had wished for her children to run on in abandon. When she sees a photo of the children she thinks, how familiar, how familiar these children in their clothes and their faces, as though she could open a door and see them standing there with their voices and their little feet.

On a cold night

Huddled by the hearth, staring at the cold grate: *Ignite!* she wills, *Ignite!* And now the flames are catching, racing, burning back, through the years and through the houses and it is more than she can bear to watch.

She changes the baby

(She's left it a bit too long) chucks it out the window, hangs washing over the balcony, matching pillowcase to sheet, keeping the socks together. She can see right down to the kitchen table, the quarry-tiled floor below, the gap just wide enough for a child to slip through.

She counts the children

More keep appearing. She adds a pill to a bowl of ice, that way it goes down easier. The absurd ability to procreate! By the final count there are ten milling about the room. A real mother, she thinks, would be calm; to each she would give her full attention – no peripheral vision, no eyes in the back of her head. No panic deadline. Into whosoever's eyes, there she would be, looking. She makes her excuses this version of a mother, keeps herself out of the picture. It grieves her to leave them, these children (so well behaved). They can't all be her can they?

She has had her cup of tea

Now she's on the window ledge but the drop is too far. The dark haired woman says: *Try the other one, it's higher.*

Where are the children?

This little devil is balanced on one foot like an acrobat on a tightrope. He's taking it too far this fearlessness. She still has a hold off his hand. Tentative this hold ... *come away from the edge* ... that will not hold ... *I would strap you to me, braid you to my being.*

Little child that you are, small as ... *but two inches tall* ... *O child of mine* ... *we need to climb these stairs so steep and high, you and I.* Little devil won't comply. Look she says, picking up some bead or brick. Still he hides, not for fooling, lost to the eye. There he is! Scooting amongst the toys, so small she may never find him. Until she does, cornered in the doll's house by a stuffed monster. Grabbing a dinosaur, she hurtles it down the stairwell. *See what trouble my boy has got himself into.*

This little thing is abandoned, uncared for, in a place she has been placed (a home? an institution?) this child she has known, here in this repository. Go to her, show her things ... and there are things, all around, as in a museum ... play with her ... *here is Peter Rabbit, here a game of tiddlywinks* ... tell her when things go wrong she needs look inside herself, know that she knows what you mean. It is time to go. Here she must stay, her curled hair straight now, lank around her face. *I do not know if I have helped or harmed and it breaks my heart to leave you.*

Tomorrow deceives

Small things in their places; knowing where their places is. In her bedroom, in *all* her bedrooms – under a window, by the end of a bed, against a wall, is a gold wicker linen basket. She keeps inside the usual folded things. It's not the inside that bothers, only the wanting to replace (that it already were) the worn candy-striped fabric of the lid. Always has, always will. This she knows from her life thus far, has not the energy to dispute, nor any point can she see, even on the brightest of mornings.

She wanted to direct him

To that place in the centre of her chest where all her woe was held as if in a deep cup never drunk dry. The place she placed her hand for comfort – or two, one upon the other, a double prayer. This is where a needle should be she thinks, this is where her skin should be punctured, here, in this spot. Somewhere in there her heart lays, her disobedient heart, hearkening to all she cannot tend to in the drear of night.

In her room she imagines

Herself sitting in such a room, a darkened room, in the very same house, the house in which she lives. She imagines a son, another son, a daughter, having left (that they will) one day, for school/work/shops/ the cinema, never to return; the furniture, carpet, clothes in her wardrobe unfamiliar; the letters on the doormat addressed to someone else: that the person climbing the stairs (no likeness to friend or family) knows not of her existence.

III.

Exposure

A small island

She who never learnt to swim: clams up, cuts away her tendrils
– tender they are, all sloop and weep and dubious caress. Out
of mind is out of sight. The lonely answer. Meanings swell …
seeing is what isn't; being flips and flounders. She knows what
she hasn't been up to now. Better, later, never . . . wavering . . .
Shall she tell? Wounds keeper, finders deeper . . . deep-ends.
Take in the best spirit, beckon with a slight gesture, an inclined
head. Return to the origin, recoup, recap. What treasures to be
had . . . if only. She has a liking for salt-biscuits, something
tangy on the tongue. Kept in, occasionally protruding. A coin
between the teeth, two for the eyes with no sight.

Interpretation (3): Outing

Here is day, here is the coast, here is the wind blustering. A grill, rusted and reinforced, covers a pit to the sea. Here is rock weathered and crumbling. It is hard to push a hospital wheelchair across uneven ground; the wheels catch and swivel back. *Glad it isn't me, thinks she, pushed or pushing.* For an old person a scone broken into bits is ample. Here is day at the cliff's edge.

(Here is night engulfing day. Water gushes through an open window, leaks and flows from every possible faucet. *She sleeping thinks; waste, such utter waste!* Sheets of ice and icicles form. Here is night, it does not hide (as does she.) Watch this woman padding along the corridor: unsteady woman, weak at the knees . . . *Too late!* . . . knocks a syringe off a shelf . . . *still sleeping . . . Be careful! Oh please be careful!* Where it lands a worm scrawls, thread like. The contaminated needle is returned to the shelf. Metal beds with brown blankets are strewn across a floor of rubble and scree, from the distance she can't see – there is no rubble, there is no scree. See what night can do:

Nigh and fleet as day, straddling the shoreline. See this woman meander into the water as if on a whim to paddle . . . *at this late hour?* See her caught by the tide and swept away. Watch as she floats . . . *sleeping, still sleeping* . . . spread-eagled below the surface, white boots catching the moonlight. How sudden the shift! If someone were to make haste it may very well be possible to save her. *Not I, for I cannot swim.*)

Indisposed

Every week she watches her classmates in the swimming bath, every week indisposed: no need to get changed, no need for exposure. Eventually she needs no excuse. Does she suppose they believe her?

Her father makes a mistake

So she is Linda with an 'i', born in Burmantofts, the result of what her mother would later refer to – maybe around the same time as the doctor she begs her mother to call for the pain says *it will all be alright when you're married*, her mother having moved her into her own more perfect bedroom, her own brand-new slippers neatly by the bed – as an overrated pastime.

In the safety of your own bathroom

Fill the sink with tepid water. Take a deep breath, lower your face and then breathe out. There should be bubbles.

Part of her left eyebrow

Appears to be missing. Surely it was there the day before. The doctor prescribes cream for eczema: *Not to be used on the eyes* she reads. The eyebrow he says, has alopecia. She remembers from childhood the alien white circle on the back of her head.

The woman who gave her paperclips

Had rigid dark hair, more like a wig. She knew another woman once whose elderly mother sat in the front room with only the crossword for company. Her own mother had a front room they never used: the three-piece-suite covered in polythene, Peter Pan on the mantelpiece trapped in a plastic bag.

Look at the child

Black and white in a nurse's uniform, staring from a winged high-back chair. Look in her eyes. See how short and straight her legs are, how she sits on her hands. See the rubber plant, sparse in its corner. Spy the ribbon – or tape – or is it a tie from an apron or dress? trailing from under the cushion. Was it stuffed there in haste? Someone knew. See what is missing. What may have been.

Dancing

Can be done at anytime, mathematically speaking. A child in the front row, she sees the Prince's laddered tights. This opens up and widens her. In her grandparent's house, at the end of a terrace, up a hill you get to through Gledhow Valley Woods, next to a parade where the green-grocer has straw on the floor, she sees an advert on the television for a delicious Bounty bar and the next minute her grandfather's giving her the money and she's dancing to the sweet shop across the dual carriageway.

Her words of wisdom

To her eldest daughter, not to sit on a boy's knee at that time
of the month was all her mother ever did say on the matter,
leaving it to that book in the brown paper bag on the top shelf
of the wardrobe, the clothes each separated by plastic, the new
ones kept hanging for a great length of time, not to be spoilt
by wearing.

The word 'cowl'

Doesn't mean what she wants it to mean. This frustrates. What she wants it to mean she doesn't know, yet. Is this where hope lies, what hope is? *I'm a survivor* writes itself in big letters on the inside of her forehead. Add an exclamation mark. I am like a shell she thinks; an empty bit in the middle, everything stuck to the sides – the insides. It is remarkable or boring how far off track she can be, like a stand up comedian but not a bit funny. This is getting her nowhere she fully believes – then she remembers the caul, the amniotic membrane adhered to her sister's newborn skull.

Just like her to want to re-examine

To prod and poke (she does it so effectively) . . . *Mischief-maker*. Hark back to this: Roundhay High School For Girls; *la crème*, the dangling *carotte* – she'd be fourteen or fifteen; the Science lab (poor Miss Burden): There she sits, hair tightly curled in her mother's rollers, unperturbed – do as I dare, not as *she* says.

On a derelict patch of land . . . In a disused quarry . . . Down by The Bumps . . . In the neighbour's garage . . . Up on the earth of Gledhow Valley Woods (through which she makes her way to her grandmother's house) . . . *turns round* . . . little ones scamper, whimper . . . *and turns no more her head* . . . his skinny hands, his glittering eye . . . up jumps . . . doth close behind her tread . . . never catch me alive, said he . . . and his ghost may be heard . . .

This idea of punishment . . . (she does it to herself so effectively)

There was a girl

(whose fingers don't remember the curling, rolling, pinning – were they nimble, speedy, purposeful, deft – and what of her is left? – was it her single bravest thing?) leaning against the prow of a boat, trousers tight at the ankles; elfish (which is not in her nature), urchin. A character in her own life. She remembers a green coat, an unwelcome coat, stifling, restrictive, and a duffel bag. The cracks in her tongue, did she have them then? *Ex*, she thinks . . . meaning *gone, lost*. It stings like a barb. A barb is more piercing than a thorn; thorns occur where there are beasts, somewhere impenetrable like the past. Clusters of short, sharp spikes set at intervals; wire trained over and under, guided, twisted, knotted; ends, several of them, cut and sharp. *Don't go this way.* (She can only go the way she has.) How close *elfish* to *selfish*. Rosy-barb, tiger-barb, barbels. A hook. A slender feeler. A sharp projection at the end of an arrow. Many early child-rearing practices were barbarous by modern standards. When she wakes in the night, her sleeping mouth is parched.

Blind eye, hair lip, gammy leg

Bunions, psoriasis: corns, warts, moles, varicose veins, alopecia: blood spots, in-growing toenails. Itch and scratch privately. Prostate cancer, liver cancer, arthritis, scleroderma (this one gets her mother), paedophilia.

Not long after

The chair began to sway, its legs tapering to points, needle fine and balanced on a pin and there was she perched high. They told her she was highly-strung – she pictured herself dangling from the tallest crane. *Look at her, she's shokeling again,* her grandfather said.

Her nails continued

The daily events. Perhaps she was quieter, crouching on the staircase halfway up, fingering the frosted glass: small lumps pushing through a smooth membrane.

Not the whole finger

Just the skin: a thin epidermal layer, pared but intact, each
crease, each criss-crossed line, and the nail, scratching inside
her head, leaving its imprint – middle finger, inherited finger
(she gives hers to her daughter) – taps her on the shoulder,
prods her in the back. A gremlin whose skinny arm outreaches,
outbalancing his short squat body, a Sméagol, a toad behind
her neck? – whose after-face is her father's, tender and made
of air.

Hot water bottle

When she unscrews the stopper and pours in the hot water, squeezing out the air before she screws it back, she thinks of her thin little father doing the same for her.

IV.

Emergence

The Onlooker withholds

She has insight: too many organs, blood and guts unseemly and quivering churning about in there, the back of her mind scratched and scarred – lesions, adhesions, a vile conglomeration. Can you tell an old spleen from a young? She could visualise a cross-section of the inside of her head, sinew and muscle, the linearity of it all, detailed and labelled: content and matter reduced to terminology, but she won't allow it, she just won't.

But she can't visualise The Onlooker ... perhaps a richly woven waistcoat, billowing sleeves, dashing hair . . . a swashbuckler . . . a Pied Piper, elfin and sprightly? A genie, expanding from a narrow-necked bottle, consuming space, her space? Her creature comfort, a fob watch in his big-bellied pocket? Her antichrist? If the wind changes he'll stay that way.

Interpretation (4)

It's years since she's been and it hasn't changed a bit: A fire warms from a recess cut into the wall, burns slow and glowing. Here is a different clutter: walls papered with pictures (look – there's one of hers) surfaces laden with books. On the counter tentatively delineating kitchen from 'living' space, as though there's no place else sits a family of carvings, like miniature Henry Moore's, grand in conception, small in stature: over-large fruit, segmented, ready to be relieved of each inedible portion. Here dwells, she thinks, a *thinking* mind, not one to be bothered by the travails of housekeeping. The air is smoky from fire and tobacco. Amongst the paraphernalia – ashtray, coffee cups, newspapers – lies a grand 'neglected' tome of Italian proportions. A large bulldog clip is clamped ceremoniously over half the pages.

(The man next to her is reading a poem. She is sufficiently close (seated) to notice he reads *backwards*, starting at the last line and finishing at the first. Such originality, she comments. Turns out, he's a bit of an inventor – some sort of electrical device consisting of tangled wires and a very large bulldog clip – a newcomer, not yet established in . . . *I'm just popping over to the electrical shop* says she *to buy a light bulb* (low voltage) excusing her sudden departure, and here he is again making connections, taking the liberty of testing out his contraption, which entails crawling on all fours. Feeling the need to vouch for his credentials, she approaches the owner of the shop pointing out the prototype on the floor, beginning to explain, with no knowledge whatsoever, exactly how it works.)

Call him old-fashioned

Nameless and timeless, arms and legless – bodiless in his magnificence – and what a heart! brain fit to bursting (she's getting sentimental) all binding, bound and bonded, to her. Everyone needs a special friend. Make sure the first time you meet to let someone know where you are. Better than sorry. He's a home bird though isn't he – in the shadows, looking on.

Querist

She queries herself, constantly. Asks of herself. In this case her query (is there a body to ask?) is in its inception. As she formulates she doubts. It's a question of accuracy (the sheet folded corner to corner, the two-pounds-fifty-one-pence *exactly*). Did he have a master key or saunter in through an unlocked door? (No matter what he was wearing – what was she?). Did she call for him unawares, signal to the universe? Was she too needy, he like god watching her every move, judging her unvoiced thoughts? What she'd like is an out of body experience, to float back *then* and observe, to know beyond question. Why so long to make himself known? Could she not envisage? Could she not believe? Could she not distinguish . . . her spirit guide . . . her beloved uncle?

The story nobody told her

Her grandfather returns to tell her a story *except he doesn't.* The story he tells her *doesn't* she was told *wasn't* was told her by her uncle *except he couldn't have.* This is that story *not.*

Your (her) clothes were (are) laid out by the side of her (your) bed *supposition – her mother did do that sort of thing but that was later when she was older* red smocked dress *it was tartan* white ankle socks . . . no . . . *told you* . . . there were (are) no clothes *there was a gold angora bolero, very fluffy, got up your nose* . . . while she (you) slept (sleep) goblins *suspend belief if you haven't already* . . . no . . . little mice *whatever* took (take) pity on her (you) *because of the clothes?* stitch(ed) and sew(ed) all night long and when you (she) woke (wake) your dress, her socks, your gold angora bolero oh no! all were (are) gnawed to shreds *in a symbolic way.*

The last she saw her uncle he was mending a plug in the hallway. How old she was she does not know. She was kept off school. There were no seat belts then.

She had a different uncle

With crinkly hair – greased and black in small tight waves –
stubby fingers and a scar on his hand. When she was older she
drew a picture of him, screwed it up into a tightly scrunched
ball and jumped on it.

She was on her way

From something to something. She'd gone downstairs ignoring *cold*, but cold not ignoring her had returned for a pair of tights, her only interest that the inconvenience soon be over. It was then that she saw the floor, the floor she'd 'seen' many times before, neither here nor there but elsewhere, and she could neither grasp nor doubt it, say when or in what state she had partaken, save that it was previous – but only as far as she could tell. And then it was gone and she could only wonder.

The person she used to be

Was 'highly strung' and won a paint-blobbing competition. She has the small crisp envelope, her name on the front in her mother's neat cursive script. When she unfolds the piece of paper inside, it opens wide into a butterfly.

Says The Onlooker:

I see you are painting

And so she is, with brushes, various in breadth and temperament, dripped in mud. (To proceed she needed to know.)

It began, says she, without form – base and mired, a little relentless (she used to etch with the point of a needle), took me by surprise. I didn't question, didn't despair – difficult to sustain an interest I carried on, applied thick strokes, began to see I could begin again: from clod and clump and barren consternation a tree could be, brushed into root, to leaf, to vein; twig corresponding to lacewing, linnet, leitmotif.

Something removed, something arising

From over her shoulder he diverts her endeavours. At first her world is murky, a grimy realm, flat and cracked, conspiring to obfuscate. She doesn't mind such meddlesome ways: when he says *you need only look up*, she does from her engrossment. (It seems he is wiser than she.) Such a downpour! A fountain of colour! Where once was marsh and quicksand, a firebird flies, dips its wings in sunset, circles, calls to another.

How will you know when it's finished?

She is sufficiently close to notice he reads backwards . . .

She too has a poem to read, to an audience whom she faces. Small strips slightly wider than shredded paper curl in conspiracy around each other: on each a phrase, a fragment. There in some sense lays sense. It's not really *that* much of a puzzle, all she needs do is find the right order, extrapolate what is clearly (or not) already there. People are waiting, not just poets. She begins, hesitant, stumbling. *Stutters, stammers, could do better.* Not hers these words that dupe – so slow are they at leaving her mouth she can barely remember what came last. To construe meaning is hardly possible. Look! She says turning to face her detractors, drawing out as if from a magician's bag those symbols that confound; crafted, adorned, embellished (no flat and boring surface on which their content rests). *Here is the essence. Make of it what you will.*

Somewhere a shelf

Spine ends sunned. Edge wear and fractional bumping to corners.

Which strategy? She suspects the alphabet. Something visual? How to remember a shopping list: Walk out of your front door (hypothetically). No sooner have you stepped out than you hear a crunching sound (1. A box of eggs.) What a mess! Never mind, down the steps, neatly tripping over an orange, three of them (Item Nº 2); along the path, something crisp underfoot (3. Cereal) etc. etc. Here's the drift: no nearer, no further away.

Back-strip detached from front cover. One inch of front gutter reglued. Age-grimed.

Where could she have been! And for what purpose? She had looked and her mind had declined: Let it stay. Leave it. You have no need. Context eluding her again like a missed opportunity.

Short gift note on endpaper. No dust jacket. Numerous illustrations.

To locate again the shelf among shelves, the book among books in a room unparalleled; to lift from the shelf the cloth-backed book, to unhook it, read again the title lettered in gilt, *Things Fall Apart*; to not put it back.

Hinges cracked. Scattered foxing to prelims, fore-edge and occasionally to pages. Contents in fine condition.